IN THE SHADOW OF CALVARY: A BIBLE STUDY OF JOHN 12-17

HAYES PRESS

Copyright © 2015 HAYES PRESS

Published by:

HAYES PRESS

The Barn, Flaxlands

Royal Wootton Bassett

Swindon, SN4 8DY

United Kingdom

www.hayespress.org

I0200899

CHAPTER ONE: THE REJECTED KING (EDWIN NEELY)

———

In a sense, the whole of eternity sits in the shadow of Calvary. Never was there, nor will there be, a more important event than the shedding of the blood of Christ, who through the eternal Spirit offered Himself without blemish unto God. Calvary is the fulcrum of human history, prophesied in early Genesis; central to the whole of Scripture, even the future in Revelation; and to the theme of praise and worship in the present, both here and in heaven. This book, however, confines itself to the events and teachings that transpired from the entrance of Christ into Bethany, John 12:1, to His final recorded supplication prior to Gethsemane, in John 17.

By the weekend of that entrance into Bethany, the sixty-nine weeks of Daniel's prophecy (Daniel 9:25) had all but run their course, after which Messiah was to be cut off. Four hundred and eighty-three years previously, Artaxerxes' command to rebuild Jerusalem (Nehemiah 2:6) had excited the builders from Babylon to return. Since Peter's declaration that no matter what men in general thought, Jesus is the Christ, the Son of the living God, Jesus had been showing His disciples that He must go up to Jerusalem and suffer, and be killed, and be raised up the third day (Matthew 16:21). Then He left Galilee for the last time, not to return there until after His resurrection. Now, this final week brings the culmination of all that these other things led up to, the fulfilment of divine purpose in the incarnation.

It is not our purpose to attempt a harmony of the Gospels for this final week, except to reflect that all the Scriptures are true, and if hard for us to place in time sequence, it is we, not they, who are at fault. We shall confine our thought to matters recorded in John, which have particular

1

importance when viewed in relation to their proximity to the death of the Lord Jesus Christ.

The Scene at Bethany

THERE MAY BE SOME FRUITFUL comparison between the specific days that began the ministry of Christ that are mentioned in the first two chapters of John and the six days that are outlined here at the end of His ministry. Certainly He did some things in those early days which are repeated here: His baptism and its counterpart in His death; the cleansing of the temple; and His appearing at a special dinner. Indeed, there seems to be a development worthy of note in the meals that He is recorded to have attended in this Gospel. At Cana, He began as guest; in John 12:1 He is guest of honour; on the beach in John 21 He is the host. Our own lives would show growth if we allowed Him the same progress in them. As John said, "He must increase, but I must decrease".

This Bethany supper is the first mentioned opportunity for us to see the reunited family together after the resurrection of Lazarus. One notices the great similarity between the activities of that lovely trio before and after that occasion. Martha served; Mary sat at His feet; Lazarus, His friend, sat at table with Him; all graphically depicting a truth that is elsewhere emphasized in Scripture; our position and service after resurrection will be related to that which we have developed in life (cf. Matthew 19:27-30; Matthew 25:21; Luke 19:24; 2 Timothy 2:11). Often throughout their lives would those gathered at that meal remember their fellowship with the Master, and many a time, no doubt, would the sweetness of that remembrance lighten the burden of the moment.

More than once in His lifetime had the Lord been anointed with precious perfume, and each occasion recorded (perhaps there had been many more) is rich in its teaching. But this anointing by Mary takes on a special significance because of its timing. Mary loved her brother Lazarus, yet that precious spikenard had not been used on his body, so recently dead. It was the anticipation of the Lord's burial that caused the sweetness to flow. Mary seemed to have an insight into the matter beyond even that of His apostles, perhaps gained in her hours spent at the Lord's feet. But her action was more than anticipatory. Mary identified herself with both His death and burial, not only by anointing Him, but by wiping His feet with her hair. It may have been a most unconventional thing for a Jewish woman to loose her hair in the presence of men, but convention gave place to devotion, and the whole house was filled with the fragrance.

There was to be no shortage of ointments and spices for His burial. Much of it, because it was brought too late, would never be used for the purpose. Yet a seeming surfeit of sweetness is no reason for not bringing the gift, a point underscored by the Lord's stout defence of Mary's action. His statement about the lasting nature of the matter, that it would be told wherever the gospel would be preached worldwide, shows the importance He placed upon it. Perhaps I would do well to remind myself of this at the remembrance and prayer meetings when I seem to have difficulty offering what I have stored up during the week.

Public Reaction

WE ARE NOT TOLD HOW many guests had been invited to this supper. Bethany by the meaning of its name was associated with food, and whether at the home of Mary and Martha, or at the home of Simon the Leper, Scripture refers to hospitality freely given. During that last week it is probable that all twelve disciples, plus any women that followed along to minister to the group, were cared for here. Bethany may well have been the place to which many of the disciples fled after the arrest in Gethsemane. In any case, a great multitude of the Jews, hearing that Jesus was there, came out of curiosity, not only to see Him, but to see Lazarus whom He had raised from the dead a short time before. Contrasted with this interest and the attention shown by those who had been with Him when Lazarus was raised and who were willing to testify to the reality of it all (v.17), were the chief priests, many of them Sadducees who did not believe in even the possibility of resurrection.

The hatred of these latter was spurred on by the fact that the resurrection of Lazarus was turning many to follow Christ. Such is the power of resurrection life. Yet despicable as the official attitude was, it was superseded in heinous character by the greed of Judas. It was not that Jesus had no care for the poor, for when Judas left the Passover feast a few days later, some thought that he had been sent to give money to the poor from the communal purse. But recognizing, as indeed Mary also must have done, that poverty would continue to characterize not only the world around, but those who would be "with you" (see Deuteronomy 15:11), and that there would be limited time to give such devotion to the Master, Christ defended her action. When good is prompted, evil often presents itself, but Scripture so often used this to show the beauty of that which is precious to God. So the preciousness of Mary's action stands out in great contrast to the depravity of Judas' evil. Moreover what Judas began in his carping criticism, others took up, swelling his condemnation (Mark 14:4). Murmuring is so contagious!

The Presentation of the King

ON THE DAY FOLLOWING, the multitude from Bethany was met by the throng from Jerusalem coming to meet the One of whom they had heard. To these Jesus presented Himself as King: "Rejoice greatly, O daughter of Zion! Shout in triumph, O daughter of Jerusalem! Behold, your King is coming to you; He is just and having salvation, Lowly, and riding on a donkey, A colt, the foal of a donkey" (Zechariah 9:9). The humility of the Saviour riding upon the back of the lowly donkey was matched by His tenderness in taking along the mother of that unbroken colt, and His unwillingness to show less than due care for the animals (Mark 11:3): "And immediately He will send it here." No loss accrues to those who give for the Master's use.

The hosannas of the day would be matched by the praises of the children on the following day. We are reminded that so very often the actions of the parents are reflected in their young. In this case the children fulfilled Scripture, Psalm 8:2: "Out of the mouth of babes and nursing infants, You have ordained strength." When the Lord reminded those who chided Him about this scripture, those who knew their Bibles must have smarted at the context of these verses that He had quoted to them. Perhaps these shouts of those who praised were part of the antiphonal recitation of Psalm 118:25-26. Poignant indeed the context of these words also: "The stone which the builders rejected has become the chief corner stone" (v.22). And: "Bind the festival sacrifice with cords to the horns of the altar" (v.27).

In spite of what has been called the triumphal entry of Christ into Jerusalem, He did not come to be accepted as King. The fickle praises poured upon Him that day would soon clash with the cacophony of mob hatred. He must be rejected. And resulting from that rejection would come His own rejection of Israel. Key verses in John's gospel say this: "He came to His own, and His own did not receive Him. But as many as received Him, to them He gave the right to become children of God, to those who believe in His name" (John 1:11-12). From the time of the praises of adults and children, there would arise discord in continuing strength until that dissonance carried the day. Yet arising out of the discord of the evil hearts of men comes a song of greater sweetness and strength, our own harmony of praise to the One who has through His rejection and death made Himself worthy to be our King: "You are my God, and I will praise You; You are my God, I will exalt You. Oh, give thanks to the LORD, for He is good; For His mercy endures forever" (Psalm 118:28,29).

CHAPTER TWO: THE LAST PUBLIC APPEARANCES (TREVOR SANDS)

———

In our reading of the gospels, we can find certain incidents on the Lord's journey to the cross which must have brought great joy to His troubled pathway. May I suggest that the request of the Greeks to "see Jesus" was one of these. The twelfth chapter of John's gospel so clearly shows us the bitter hatred of the Jewish leaders and the shallow response of the multitude to the Lord's teaching and signs. Just as in His earliest days it was Gentile wise men who enquired for Israel's King so, at the close of His public ministry, Greeks asked to see Israel's Saviour. How beautifully the words concerning them in John 12:20 - "those that went up to worship" - express a far deeper conviction than that possessed by the majority of Jews in Jerusalem that Passover week; who, one fears, had simply "come to the feast" (12:12).

Much speculation has taken place as to how the Lord's reply relates to this sincere Gentile request. An early legend suggested that the Greeks were a deputation offering Him political asylum out of His enemies' reach, but there is no evidence for such an explanation. Is it not more natural to think that the sight of worshipping Gentiles led on to the glorious prospect of a redeemed people gathered together from every nation as a kingdom and priests and thus to the cost to Him of such a redemption to God (Revelation 5:9-10). Let us look then, in a little more detail, at the Lord's teaching concerning His work of redemption.

The Son of Man Glorified

IT IS IMPORTANT TO distinguish between the glory of the returning victorious One, ascended to the Father's right hand (see, for example, 1

Peter 1:21) and the glory of that dreadful "hour" of suffering. A careful reading of Hebrews 2:9 helps us to see beyond the thorn-crowned Man whom men cast out, to the Man crowned with glory and honour, casting out the prince of this world from his wrongful domain (John 12:31). How little of God's purposes even the disciples understood will become clear in subsequent chapters in this book. The magnificent divine promise of the glory to be brought to God's Name fell perhaps not surprisingly then on a deafened multitude (John 12:28). Some mistook the voice of God for the voice of nature. Others mistook the Creator's voice for that of the created being. From its belief in uncontrolled evolutionary forces to its ridicule of Holy Scripture, our own generation too is deaf to the voice of God in the glorious work of His Son.

The Grain of Wheat Dead

THE SECOND ASPECT OF the Lord's redemptive work brought before us in this passage shows us clearly how the plan of creation and the plan of redemption were framed in the same Mind: both in perfect harmony, one beautifully foreshadowing the other. On the third day of creation (see Genesis 1:11), God Himself ordained the method by which much of plant life should propagate and increase. As with all the divine ways, this was no arbitrary choice. Accustomed as we are to the created order of things, we may think it could not have been otherwise. Yet an Almighty Creator could have chosen any method He wished to multiply a species. But, even as the first grain of wheat fell into the ground, it was a picture of events still far in the future. The Word of God, as He made all things, knew even then, before man sinned, that He was THE grain of wheat who would fall into the ground and die. How wonderful in a future day to see the great "wheat-fields" which have come from that one precious grain - much more wonderful to be a small part of the "much fruit" of the work of Calvary.

The Son of Man Lifted Up from the Earth

IN THE INCIDENT OF John chapter 21 the shoal of 153 fish which had evaded the nets of experienced fishermen all the night were drawn by the Master's command to the shore that morning. The teaching of the Lord to the Jews in John chapter 6 was, "No man can come to Me, except the Father which sent Me draw him" (John 12:44). Again, how different from the world's view of a crucified Man as powerless and defeated. Even the most powerful and victorious of men are able to find salvation only as they are drawn by the crucified Saviour. How aptly the multitude's response (John 12:34) illustrates the truth of 1 Corinthians 1:18 - "For the message of the cross is foolishness to those that are perishing".

Having thought briefly of some facets of the Lord's redemptive work, it may be profitable now to consider the possible responses to His invitation and claims from the standpoint of His glorious title: "light of the World".

Believe on the Light

AMIDST ALL THE DIFFICULT teachings of the Pharisees, the political subversion of the Zealots, the compromising philosophy of the Herodians and all else that Jerusalem's inhabitants and visitors were daily subjected to, the simplicity of the divine message was indeed "light shining in darkness". Down the centuries since, many have stumbled in the darkness rather than humble themselves to "believe on the light" and thus become "sons of light". To any readers who are puzzled as to how to receive light in these dark days, we would commend to you our Master's words as the only way of salvation.

The Consequence of Light Rejected

IN ISRAEL'S TIME OF slavery in Egypt, the Pharaoh of that day set himself up against Almighty God and refused to let God's people go and worship. He continually hardened his heart (e.g. Exodus 8:32). Until one day his opportunity to believe God's word through Moses and Aaron was over and then "The LORD hardened the heart of Pharaoh" (Exodus 9:12). Similarly, in John 12 we see that those who had continually heard the words of grace from "a greater than Moses" eventually "could not believe". Their day of opportunity was over. As well as being a fearful warning to unsaved ones who like hard rocks beneath the sea continually let the gospel wash over them, this passage also has a solemn voice for the believer.

God has given much tight in His Word for disciples, longing that they might be obedient to His revealed will. If, however, we are not willing to accept this light immediately perhaps because of its cost to us in terms of changed lifestyle or breaking of old unscriptural associations - we cannot presume that God will always show us such light. Once saved, we can never lose our eternal security, but what a loss of present happiness and eternal reward will be ours if we prefer our own dark pathways to the light of God's ways.

The Hidden Light

IT IS EASY TO SEE IN these verses the example of men who lit a lamp and hid it instead of putting it on a stand (see Matthew 5:15). Rather than being smug or criticizing these men, as we read in these verses, may God help us to examine our own lives. The consequences of letting their light shine would be severe; being put out of the synagogue was the end of all social respectability and much more to the Jew. With us, is it just that we "like to be liked" that prevents us making the remark which shows we have God's light within us? To hide our light is shown up in

John 12:43 for what it really is - not timidity, shyness or anything which sounds so excusable. The reality is we love the flickering fading glory of men more than the surpassing weight of God's glory.

Conclusion

AS WE COME TO THE END of John 12 we read the Lord's closing words to unbelieving Israel before He gives His precious teaching to His loved and His own. How they should have been moved as His perfect obedience to His Father's will brought to mind their long national history of waywardness and unbelief. In beholding the Son they could behold the Father (v.45). In listening to the Son they could hear the Father (vv.49,50). Only by believing on the Son, could their much vaunted belief in the Father be shown to have any substance whatsoever (verse 44). As disciples of the lord Jesus Christ, surely the Son must have the preeminent place in our hearts and lives because of all that He has done for us.

"Let us run with endurance the race that is set before us, looking unto Jesus, the author and finisher of our faith, who for the joy that was set before Him endured the cross, despising the shame, and has sat down at the right hand of the throne of God" (Hebrews 12:1-2).

CHAPTER THREE: AN OBJECT LESSON IN HUMILITY (BOB ARMSTRONG)

The Setting

"Jesus, knowing that the Father had given all things into His hands, and that He had come from God and was going to God, rose from supper and laid aside His garments, took a towel and girded Himself. After that, He poured water into a basin and began to wash the disciples' feet, and to wipe them with the towel with which He was girded." (John 13:3-5).

There is no record, as they travelled in Israel for three years, that any of the disciples ever washed the feet of Christ, no doubt often travel-stained and weary. To a woman, deeply repentant of her sins, goes the honour of such an act. In the house of Simon the Pharisee she quietly stood behind Him, tears flowing, sufficient to bathe His feet, which she dried with her hair and kissed repeatedly (Luke 7:36-50).

A quote from the book "Bible Lands Customs" is helpful about feet washing. "After bowing, greeting, and kissing, the Eastern guest is offered water for washing his feet. A servant will assist the guest by pouring the water on his feet over a copper basin, rubbing the feet with his hands, and wiping them with a napkin". This was confirmed by the Lord's censure of Simon: "Do you see this woman? I entered your house; you gave Me no water for My feet, but she has washed My feet with her tears and wiped them with the hair of her head. You gave Me no kiss, but this woman has not ceased to kiss My feet since the time I came in" (Luke 7:44-45).

Water was provided by the host and only when a menial servant was present were the feet washed by such a person. This explanation greatly enhances the Lord's selfless action on the betrayal night. He took the place of the servant to minister. Had He not taught the disciples earlier, "whoever desires to become great among you, let him be your minister [Greek: diakonos – servant]. And whoever desires to be first among you, let him be your slave [Greek: doulos – bondservant]". Our Lord then added: "just as the Son of Man did not come to be served, but to serve (diakonos), and to give His life a ransom for many" (Matthew 20:28).

The Action

IN THE UPPER ROOM SCENARIO that historic night, we see the astonished disciples with uncomprehending eyes watch their Lord and Master remove His outer garment, wrap a towel around His body, pour water into a basin, then one by one tenderly wash their feet... until He came to Peter. "Lord, are You washing my feet" (John 13:6)? It was as much an assertion as a question, because Peter had already made up his mind. One marvels at the way the Lord handled Peter's interruption so gently. "What I am doing you do not understand now, but you will know after this" (John 13:7).

Peter, impulsive, self-assertive, was not satisfied with Christ's reply and blurted out, "You shall never wash my feet!" (v.8). The others listened in shocked silence. It was like a stinging rebuke to Christ. Peter, how could you dare say that to the Lord? However much we may wish to make allowance for Peter, that he must have felt so inferior to the Lord, it still comes across as Peter's will against the Lord's. The fact remains on the record that he talked back to the Sovereign Lord of the universe!

As we reconstruct the scene we feel a deep sense of worship before the lord, for His amazing humility and patience with Peter in his blundering refusal. However, before condemning the fledgling apostle, can we not see a reflection of our own nature in moments of self-will, to win a point, or justify an action? The tragedy of this is that we may do it in the Name of the Lord. Is it not true that sometimes we walk a thin line between God's glory and our own glory? However strongly we may contend for God's will and glory, it should never violate the spirit of meekness and humility.

In the room that night, right under the shadow of Calvary, a contrary human will co-existed with divine humility of amazing dimensions. The break came when the Lord quietly told Peter, "If I do not wash you, you have no part with Me" (John 13:8). The Greek word for "part" is "meros", meaning a section or allotment, a division or share. At that moment, it threatened to be all over for Peter, not his eternal life, but his future days of service for Christ. He was standing in the way of his apostleship. That did it. He may have suddenly remembered Moses, who in anger smote the rock in Kadesh instead of speaking to it, and was denied entrance into the Promised Land.

For whatever reasons, which the Lord knew all too well, Peter quickly changed position and said, "Lord, not my feet only, but also my hands and my head". It was all or nothing. How could he have changed so quickly? Some might have said, "that man will never make it as an apostle of Christ, or of the church". Others, "he could never be commended for the work of the Lord", yet 50 days later he led the evangelism outreach in Jerusalem at Pentecost, when three thousand were saved, baptized and added to the first church of God in the new age of the Spirit. Amazing grace of God!

The Purpose

GOING BACK TO THE LORD'S words to Peter, "If I do not wash you, you have no part with Me", shows that there was more to it than simply washing the disciples' feet. The Lord adopted a cultural custom to illustrate deeper spiritual truths. Firstly, the Lord said to Peter, "He who is bathed needs only to wash his feet, but is completely clean; and you are clean, but not all of you" (meaning Judas). Two important Greek words occur here. The word "bathed" is "louo", meaning to bathe the whole body. The word "wash" is "nipto", meaning part bathing, the hands, feet or face. It was as though the Lord gave advance lessons on Paul's letter to Titus: "Not by works of righteousness which we have done, but according to His mercy He saved us, through the washing of regeneration and renewing of the Holy Spirit" (Titus 3:5).

That answers to "he who is bathed", a once-for-all washing, which takes place at the new birth. Then the ancient Scripture writer asks the question, "How can a young man cleanse his way? By taking heed according to Your word." (Psalm 119:9). This answers to the daily cleansing of the word on the walk of the disciple on his way to glory. This again is not the same as the cleansing referred to in 1 John 1:7, where it says, "the blood of Jesus Christ His Son, cleanses us from all sin."

Secondly, we read in John 13:12: "So when He had washed their feet, taken His garments, and sat down again, He said to them, "Do you know what I have done to you?" He then explained another vital principle: "If I then, your Lord and Teacher, have washed your feet, you also ought to wash one another's feet. For I have given you an example, that you should do as I have done to you." (vv. 14-15).

John's gospel deals in fundamental spiritual teaching as well as narrative. That he only of the four gospel writers records the washing of the disciples' feet, suggests it was as much a symbolic act as something He told them to do. It was not however, to be a church practice as some hold it to be. By doing it Himself He taught the disciples His own selfless humility. To actually see the humble self-effacing Christ wash their feet was far more effective than a thousand sermons on humility. They would never forget it.

Proverbs 15:33 tells us that, "The fear of the Lord is the instruction of wisdom, and before honor is humility." The disciples had to learn that spiritual principle deep in their hearts, as they set out to make disciples, plant churches, and feed the flock of God. "And a servant of the Lord must not quarrel but be gentle to all, able to teach, patient, in humility correcting those who are in opposition ..." (2 Timothy 2:24-25).

Finally, the Lord's act of humility was predictive of His own redemptive work. Years later Paul wrote:

> "Let this mind be in you which was also in Christ Jesus, who, being in the form of God, did not consider it robbery to be equal with God, but made Himself of no reputation, taking the form of a bondservant, and coming in the likeness of men. And being found in appearance as a man, He humbled Himself and became obedient to the point of death, even the death of the cross" (Philippians 2:5-8).

We must remember that although the Lord stooped to wash the disciples' feet, signifying His great descent and humbling of Himself, He gave up none of His essential Deity. Stooping to that humble task He was still God "in the likeness of men". His obedience unto death did not mean that death has power over Him. "Unto" is said to be a translation of a word that means "Up to the point of dying" (Wuest). That helps us to understand what the Lord meant when He said, "I lay down My life that I may take it again. No one takes it from Me, but I lay it down of Myself. I have power to lay it down, and I have power to take it again. This command I have received from My Father" (John 10:17-18). He was Sovereign Lord of life and death!

Humility was always in the character of our Lord as God the Son. He has left us His beautiful example of humility. Pride, the opposite to humility, is in our fallen nature, and only as we reckon it crucified with the flesh can we win the battle against pride. Pride can subtly masquerade in pseudo-humility. It's carnal, born of the flesh. God hates it. "Everyone proud in heart is an abomination to the Lord ... pride goes before destruction, and a haughty spirit before a fall" (Proverbs 16:5,18).

Many a promising spiritual life has been ruined for God, and many a preacher's message robbed of its power through secret pride in the heart. Beware of pride, Satan's trap, and who of us has not felt its power. "Yes, all of you be submissive to one another, and be clothed with humility, for "God resists the proud, but gives grace to the humble" (1 Peter 5:5). The seasoned apostle who wrote that had come a long way since the night of the historic feet-washing. Blessed be the Lord!

CHAPTER FOUR: THE TRAGEDY OF JUDAS (DON McCUBBIN)

―――

Judas was an honourable name, being derived from Judah, who became head of the royal tribe in Israel. Subsequently, it was the name of a great Jewish leader, Judas Maccabeus, who in 165 B.C. routed the Seleucid army which had profaned the Temple in Jerusalem. Since Judas was a popular name in New Testament times, a further designation was required, such as Judas, the son of James (Acts 1:13).

One of the Twelve

THE PRESENT SUBJECT is Judas Iscariot, who was also called the son of Simon. The meaning of Iscariot is not certain, but it is generally considered to be "a man of Kerioth". Kerioth was a place in Judea, so Judas could be the only one of the twelve apostles who did not come from Galilee. Nothing is known about him before he was chosen by Jesus to be one of the apostles. What led Judas initially to become a follower of the Teacher from Galilee is not known. He could well have been impressed by the miracles, if not the teaching of Christ. When many other disciples turned away from following Him (John 6:66) Judas persisted, perhaps sharing a common hope among the Jews of a place of importance in the coming Messianic kingdom.

There is no evidence that he was a Zealot or nationalist, or that Judas was not accepted by the other apostles. He could have kept himself rather separate, perhaps feeling somewhat superior to the Galileans. Subsequent events show that he could act in complete secrecy from the others. He had ability, as he was given the job of treasurer of the company, and left to dispense the funds. In the list of the names of the

Twelve, the order varies slightly, but Judas is always placed last, with the infamous stigma of the one who betrayed the Lord (Matthew 10:4). The choice of Judas was deliberate, for the Lord knew each one, including the one who would betray Him. This choice showed the amazing grace of Christ, that He could live for those years, with the knowledge of which one would turn against Him so treacherously.

Despite this, Judas was sent out with the rest of the apostles to preach the message of the kingdom, to heal the sick, cleanse those with leprosy, and drive out demons (Matthew 10:7,8). Nothing particular is known about his activities during this period, except that he pilfered the money that was entrusted to his care (John 12:6).

At Bethany

SHORTLY BEFORE THE last Passover, Jesus came to Bethany where a supper was prepared for Him. During supper Mary, the sister of Martha and Lazarus, took her treasured possession, a precious ointment, and used it all on the Lord's feet. Mary took the opportunity to express her love and devotion for Him, even to wiping His feet with her hair. Judas was incensed, and could only see the act as an extravagant waste. So he dared to criticize openly this lovely action, and having quickly assessed the value of the ointment, he complained that it could have been sold, and the money given to the poor, when in fact he would have been able to steal the money. Jesus only mildly rebuked Judas, declaring that the anointing was for His burial.

The Upper Room

WHILE THE OTHERS WERE left pondering on the reference to His burial, Judas proceeded to add deceit to his covetousness. He went off straight away to the chief priests to offer to deliver Jesus into their hands (Matthew 26:14-16). The rulers had already commanded that anyone who knew where Jesus was should disclose it, so they gladly accepted this offer and gave Judas thirty pieces of silver. This was a paltry sum, but perhaps Judas looked for more later. He may have had high hopes of becoming treasurer in the new kingdom of God, but he was now disillusioned and turned away to the power of Satan (John 13:2).

The location of the Upper Room was kept a secret, so that the Lord and His disciples would not be disturbed, for He had much to teach them even at that late hour. Not least they were to be warned of the coming betrayal, so that they would not be overwhelmed when it happened, but they would realize that even this was part of the divine plan. A touching illustration is taken from David's experience, which says "Even, mine own familiar friend, in whom I trusted, who ate My bread, has lifted up his heel against Me" (Psalm 41:9). To eat bread signified a close friendship and loyalty, and to lift up the heel is to behave like a rebellious animal, who wounds his owner. This action was fully accepted by the Lord as part of the plan to redeem mankind, and He was ready to pay the price. He was going to die at the appointed time and place. They would understand all this in a future day, when they would be sent out as His witnesses.

As they proceeded with the Passover meal, Jesus became troubled in His spirit, and He again referred to the traitor. Still no suspicion was aroused about Judas, for his deceitfulness was well covered from the other disciples. The usual arrangement for the meal has been described by Edersheim. A number of couches were placed in a U-shape round the table; the guests then reclined on the couches, lying on their left sides, and supporting themselves on their left elbows, so their right hand was free to take the food. Jesus as the host would be in the centre of the chief couch, with the main places of honour on either side.

We are told that "the disciple whom Jesus loved", who is generally considered to be John, was on the right side; so that he could rest on the breast of Jesus. We cannot be certain of the placing of the rest of the apostles, for while Peter might be expected to have a place near the Lord, he must have been some distance away, as he needed to signal to John to find out what Jesus was saying. Judas, however, was near to Jesus, so that they could speak without others hearing, and they were able to dip in the bowl together. Maybe the Lord chose Judas to take the other honoured place, so that He could make one last loving appeal to stop Judas from taking the final step.

The other disciples were perplexed at the further reference to the betrayal, obviously thinking that one of them would make some involuntary action. So they asked in turn "Lord, is it I?", but when it came to Judas he could only say, "Rabbi, Is it I?", which showed that he did not recognize Jesus as Lord (Matthew 26:21-25). Jesus answered by an action, for it would be the one who dipped in the bowl with Him. Then the giving of the sop, probably a piece of meat, would be understood as a mark of honour. However, Satan had now entered Judas and was controlling his actions.

No further appeal could succeed, so Jesus in sorrow said, "What you are about to do, do quickly" (John 13:27 NIV). So far there was no indication that the betrayal was imminent. So Judas left to carry out the treachery without the other disciples realizing what he was about to do. John says that it was night when Judas went out; this was not just physical darkness, for it was the time of the full moon, but the time of spiritual darkness which comes to all those who turn their back on the Lord. John may have had this in mind when he later wrote "If we say that we have fellowship with Him, and walk in darkness, we lie and do not practice the truth. But if we walk in the light as He is in the light, we have fellowship with one another, and the blood of Jesus Christ His Son cleanses us from all sin" (1 John 1:6-7).

The Garden of Gethsemane

THE RULERS DID NOT want to arrest and hold Jesus at the time of the feast for fear of a riot, and the inevitable reaction by the Roman army. However, when Judas arrived at the house of the high priest with the information that Jesus could be secretly arrested, their plans were altered, showing the divine overruling. How could the rulers persuade Pilate to hold a trial at the time of the feast, and how could they give evidence without defiling themselves, and when could the sentence be carried out? This would cause lengthy discussions, involving other members of the Sanhedrim. While these discussions were taking place in the city, the Lord had time to finish His teaching, and go out to Gethsemane, where He could pray to His Father as the disciples slept.

It would be very late before the Jewish leaders completed their plans, and were ready to proceed with the armed guard to make the arrest. They may have gone by way of the Upper Room in case the lord was still there, which could account for the mysterious incident of the young man who followed, and then fled naked to avoid arrest (Mark 14:51,52). When the arrest party arrived at the Garden they found Jesus not hiding away, but going out to meet them. John makes no reference to Judas giving the kiss of identification.

The synoptic Gospels record that Judas kissed Him affectionately (Marshall), while again calling Jesus, Master; but was this action necessary, for Jesus must have been well known after His clashes in the Temple? Judas presumably returned with the arrest party, but there is no reference to his taking part in the trial; evidently he must have remained nearby to hear the sentence. This completely disillusioned man, overcome by remorse, tried to return the money, but there was no undoing the act of treachery, and therefore he despairingly took his own life.

The Tragedy

SOME HAVE FELT THAT there was more in Judas' betrayal than avarice, for the reward was low. Perhaps he thought that Jesus could be made to show his power, for what limit was there for One who could even raise the dead? He could call down legions of angels to rout the Roman army, and then He could set up His Messianic kingdom. Whatever were the ultimate motives of Judas he became controlled by Satan to betray the Lord, and for this there was no forgiveness, and so Judas went to his own place (John 17:12; Acts 1:25). The tragedy of Judas was that he tried to use Jesus to better his own ends. The Master was going to conquer the power of evil, not by force, but by the way of the cross; and so "to reconcile all things to Himself...having made peace through the blood of His cross" (Colossians 1:20).

CHAPTER FIVE: THIS DO IN REMEMBRANCE OF ME (RON HICKLING)

A Darkening Shadow

In Matthew 16 we read of events which took place in the area of Caesarea Philippi. The Lord asked His disciples, "who do you say that I am?" Peter's assured and forthright answer was, "You are the Christ, the Son of the living God" (Matthew 16:16). The Gospel writer then tells us, "From that time Jesus began to show to His disciples that He must go to Jerusalem, and suffer many things from the elders and chief priests and scribes, and be killed, and be raised the third day." (Matthew 16:21). During the days of His flesh the hour of the cross was ever before the Lord (see Matthew 11:22,23; 20:17-19) yet, as He warned His disciples about what lay ahead, and although they were "exceedingly sorrowful" (Matthew 17:23), they failed to grasp the full significance of what their Master had told them.

Time passed and the shadow of the cross grew more and more pronounced. As His hour approached the Lord was troubled in His soul (John 12:27), yet His prayer was that God's Name should be glorified (John 12:28). The fact that one of His disciples would betray Him lay heavily upon His spirit (John 13:21). His familiar friend was going to lift up his hand against Him. The Lord Jesus had spoken of His death both plainly and symbolically (John 3:14; Matthew 16:21), and the time when He must leave His disciples was approaching rapidly. He spoke to his disciples about it when He said, "A little while longer the light is with you" (John 12:35). It was a time of deep sadness.

The Upper Room

THEN CAME THE FIRST day of the Feast of Unleavened Bread. The disciples enquired of the Lord where they should prepare the feast and He gave clear instructions to Peter and John to follow a man bearing a pitcher of water. He would lead them to a house with a furnished Upper Room where they were to make ready.

Later, the Lord with the rest of the Twelve followed. The city of Jerusalem would be thronged with pilgrims who had travelled there for the Passover and Jesus and His disciples would need to thread their way through the crowds. It was the custom of the Roman authority to draft more soldiers into the city on such occasions in case there should be any uprising on the part of the Jews. As the Lord and His own made their way through the streets they may well have seen, here and there evidences of the power of Gentile rule. So they came to the Upper Room.

The quiet of that chamber must have contrasted sharply with the noise outside. Not long before, the Jewish leaders had held their clandestine meeting with Judas Iscariot and the terrible bargain for Christ's betrayal had been struck (Matthew 26:14-16). How keen they were to take this Man who had spoken against them so boldly! But they had feared the multitudes and this act must be done surreptitiously (Matthew 21:45-46).

Elsewhere, outside that room, the busy world was going about its business. Away in far off Rome, great Caesar was wielding his imperial power, represented at that time in Judea by Pontius Pilate, who soon at great eternal cost and with dreadful significance would yield to the cry of the crowd and put the courting of his emperor's favour above all else (John 19:12-16). To many, very many, that little group gathered in that room meant nothing. Yet there, reclining with His own was the incarnate Son of God. Only a few hours, and the gloom of Gethsemane would become a reality, and then alone He would go to Calvary to become the great atoning Sacrifice. The types and shadows of a past day were all to be fulfilled in Him, God's promises were to be kept (Genesis 3:15). The fullness of the time had come.

It was with particular desire that the Lord had wished to eat the Passover with His disciples (Luke 22:15), for it was to be, as He expressed it, "before I suffer". With Him at that feast was a remarkable company of men of different backgrounds and characters: Simon Peter was there, that impetuous but most likeable man. Soon he would deny his Lord, only quickly to repent and afterwards suffer much in His service. Andrew, who had brought Peter to Jesus, was present. Thomas was with them, he who afterwards was to have doubts which would be swept away when he saw the signs of the Calvary wounds in His Master's resurrected body. Then there was John, a young man so dearly loved by the Lord. The rest of the Twelve were there. But they were not all clean (John 13:10-11) for amongst them, but only for a time, was the traitor who would soon receive the sop and go out to perform his dastardly deed which was to end for him in eternal night.

They were all different in so many respects yet one characteristic was common to them all; they were all mortal men. Their life with the Lord must have made a tremendous impact upon them, but being human they could easily forget. When He had gone would the memory of those days fade from their minds? And what of the multitudes who, over the centuries, were going to be reached by saving grace; how were they to remember Him whom they had never seen?

"This do ..."

AS THEY ATE THE PASSOVER together, the Lord reached out and "took bread, blessed and broke it, and gave it to the disciples and said, "Take, eat; this is My body." Then He took the cup, and gave thanks, and gave it to them, saying, "Drink from it, all of you. For this is My blood of the new covenant, which is shed for many for the remission of sins" (Matthew 26:26-28). As the disciples sat there watching and listening to the Lord they would perceive that this was something new, outside the scope of the Passover Feast, and something about which they were to learn more in the days to come, which in turn they would pass on to those who would become His disciples. It was not for the eleven alone; it was the institution of a service of remembrance to be observed by all believers who would be prepared to keep His word.

Mark, as well as Matthew, records the taking of the loaf and cup by the lord Jesus on that night, and so does Luke who tells us also that the Lord said, "Do this in remembrance of Me" (Luke 22:19). It was a clear, succinct command; it allowed for no alteration by man, there was no room to deviate. Years later, in his first letter to the saints in the Church of God in Corinth, the apostle Paul wrote about this night, telling them of how he had received his instruction from the Lord and bidding them to keep His word concerning the taking of the loaf and the cup. By so doing it would form a testimony to all who took notice, for they would be proclaiming the Lord's death. They would be looking back to the cross work, but not that only, for it was to be done "till He come". It was to point them forward also to the time when they would experience the full fruits of Christ's victory. Yet, joyous though such an ordinance was to be, it was not to be treated lightly, nor was there to be participation in it unless first there was self-examination before the Lord with confession of sin and cleansing (1 Corinthians 11:23-28).

The words "do this in remembrance of Me" call for careful consideration. It was not simply a matter of "remember Me" but "do this in remembrance of Me". It is possible to remember the Lord at any time as one meditates in private on Him, but this was the institution of a corporate act of remembrance which was to be carried out by believers gathered together for this purpose according to the divine pattern. They were to do as the Lord had done by taking bread, giving thanks, breaking it and partaking of it. The loaf was still bread and the wine still wine, but although simple ordinary substances they symbolize that which is divine and profound, as the hymn says: "Only bread and only wine, Yet to faith the solemn sign, Of the heavenly and divine".

The loaf speaks of His body and the cup of His blood. As we take the symbols we remember how He took the body which had been prepared for Him (Hebrews 10:5-7) and in which He dwelt among men bringing blessing. Yet that body was marred more than that of any man and in it He bore our sins upon the tree. The cup reminds us of the precious blood which was shed to pay for our redemption (1 Peter 2:24; 1:18-19), and points to the forgiveness received by believing ones.

Keeping the Ordinance

IN THE ACTS OF THE Apostles we read how the command of the Lord concerning the remembrance was obeyed by disciples gathered together in churches of God. From Acts 2:41-42, we learn those who received the word of life were baptized and added to those already together forming the Church of God in Jerusalem. They continued steadfastly in the apostles' teaching, the Fellowship, in the breaking of bread and the prayers.

This was true, too, of the disciples in Troas (Acts 20:7) and from this Scripture we find that the Remembrance was kept on the first day of the week. Closely associated with the breaking of the bread is the privilege, and indeed the responsibility, of those gathered together in churches of God to "enter the Holiest by the blood of Jesus..." (Hebrews 10:19-22). This is holy priesthood service when, as the people of God in the spiritual house of God, those gathered in churches of God can offer up spiritual sacrifices of worship with bowed hearts to God (1 Peter 2:5).

Sadly, as time passed the simplicity of the ordinance and purity of Scriptural teaching concerning worship was lost and men substituted their own ideas, bringing in evil doctrines and ceremonies and ritual which had no scriptural authority. Yet, in God's mercy, in comparatively recent times the Holy Spirit has exercised the hearts of many believers to search the Scriptures and seek to return to truths taught in them. So today it is still the will of the Lord that disciples should be gathered in churches of God to keep the ordinance which He instituted in the shadow of Calvary and to do so "till He come".

CHAPTER SIX: DISCIPLESHIP – ITS CHARACTER AND POTENTIAL (GEOFF HYDON)

———

L ong years before the Lord Jesus gathered with His disciples in the Upper Room, God revealed to Isaiah the situation of men in relation to Himself. He said, "As the heavens are higher than the earth, so are My ways higher than your ways and My thoughts than your thoughts" (Isaiah 55:8,9). How clearly this was demonstrated in the Upper Room dialogue. Just at the point when His thoughts seem to have been full of His impending sacrifice and the completion of the heavenly plan of salvation, the Son of God was faced with the earthly limited reasoning of His disciples. We can imagine the stunned, questioning looks on their faces as they listened to Him; His thoughts of ascension in victory translated in their minds to thoughts of abandonment and loss of position: concerns which were soon vocalized.

In this record of Upper Room events there is a reflection of the weakness found still in disciples today, but in the Lord's teaching there is a strong statement of what should really characterize them as their potential begins to be realized. Recognizing their weakness the Lord endearingly used the term "My children" (Greek: teknion) in addressing the disciples. He was reflecting on their character, relative spiritual immaturity and dependence on Him. In his first epistle, John used the same term in 1 John 2:1,12,28 when writing to those whom he saw as needing fatherly direction and care. We can certainly see the appropriateness of this description of His disciples as the Lord speaks to them in the shadow of Calvary. In this respect the conversation between the Lord and Peter, Thomas and Philip will provide us with illustrations of the needs of all disciples, then and now, to develop a Christ-like character. Our inherent weakness necessitates reliance on the Lord, and His direction will constantly call from us the daily expression of love, faith and obedience He expects.

Peter: Love and Obedience

JESUS SAW PETER'S SINCERE loyalty, but knew better than Peter just how much that loyalty was soon to be tested. Peter heard the Lord's words establishing a key characteristic of Christian disciples, namely that they should have and display the same love to each other that Christ had towards them. It seems, however, that Peter was so deeply concerned about the Master leaving them that he boldly made his loyal but rash statement of commitment, even unto death. Jesus knew that His own love, as the Good Shepherd, would cause Him to lay down His life for these sheep, but He knew Peter was not yet ready to follow Him in this fullest test of love; to give everything for others (Romans 6:7).

He also knew that Peter would recall his threefold denial of his Master when he would be challenged (after the resurrection) by the Lord's three times repeated words "Do you love Me?" Peter was to learn that the character of the disciple should be one of loving dependence on His Lord rather than on himself. How else would he be able to fulfil Christ's charge of feeding His lambs, shepherding His sheep and feeding His sheep (John 21:15-17)?

What was the potential of the disciple Peter? The Lord said to him "Will you really lay down your life for Me?" At that time he was clearly not ready to make such a sacrifice; his loyalty exceeded his resolution. But he would be ready later (2 Peter 1:14), after faithfully adhering in true disciple character to the command of the Lord to strengthen his brethren (Luke 22:32).

Thomas: Faith

THOMAS ILLUSTRATED perhaps the most noticeable problem evidenced by the disciples. It was their apparent need for a clearly described goal and a route. In response the Lord Jesus plainly declared to them that He was (and is) the Way, the Truth and the Life. They were not to receive complex directions, simply that they should stay close to Him in heart and express their love for Him by loving one another. Herein is something of the essence of Christian discipleship. Thomas, however, was looking for more tangible guidance; he is presented to us in Scripture as a man with a very black and white outlook on life. "Seeing is believing" is an expression that is associated with him and is very much in accord with today's thinking in the world at large. However, it is not in agreement with the disciple character. The Lord knew that after His crucifixion Thomas would hear His words, "see My hands" (John 20:27) because of His initial unwillingness to believe in the supremacy of spiritual power over the constraints of a human body.

In the Upper Room on that night before His passion, the Lord Jesus heard Thomas express his doubts, no doubt shared by the other disciples there, as to the mission of the Saviour. It seems he wanted a road-map of the Lord's impending journey to His glorious throne, something he could see and follow with his naked eye. He missed the point. Discipleship to Christ must be based on faith not on sight (2 Corinthians 5:7). However, Thomas would later set aside the temporal limitations to his appreciation of Jesus and proclaim Him "my Lord and my God" (John 20:28). As a direct result we now benefit from the Lord's words to Thomas, "blessed are those who have not seen and yet have believed" (v.29).

Philip: Works of Faith

PHILIP, LIKE PETER and Thomas, was trying to understand the Lord's words in a material sense. So, having explained the spiritual reality of the Father being in the Son, the Lord Jesus appealed to the material evidence of the miraculous works He had performed. Jesus had demonstrated complete faith in His God and Father to work out His will through the Son's words and actions. All the disciples had to do was exercise similar faith. Had not the Lord conveyed this same thought when He had said to Philip and the other disciples at the outset of their service, "It is enough for the student to be like his Teacher and the servant like his Master"? (Matthew 10:25). And now He adds in addressing Philip that he would have potential to do even greater things, if only he exercised that faith that should characterize those who bear the title "disciple of the Lord Jesus Christ".

Achieving Discipleship Potential

AT THIS POINT, ANOTHER of the Twelve must be brought into the picture to teach us by contrast. The apostle Peter was later to declare that Judas had "shared in this ministry" (Acts 1:17), but he did not typify it. His was a character of greed, dishonesty, hypocrisy and eventually treachery. His evil potential was fully realized when he opened his heart to provide a vehicle for Satan and he subsequently went where he belonged (Acts 1:25). His departure from the Upper Room was a necessary prerequisite to the discourse between the Lord and His true disciples on that momentous occasion. True disciples they were, despite their failings. These were men with great potential; men with a future. Christian character, as we have seen, is a developmental thing. Its basis is the initial work of the Holy Spirit and it is revealed in Christian activity through the ongoing work of the indwelling Spirit. Likewise, achieving the full potential of discipleship is subject to following the Spirit's leading in the exercise of the gifts and calling of God.

It was Christ's answer to Philip's question, "Lord, show us the Father" that contained the fullest picture of the disciples' potential. Christ had been sent from the Father to reveal Him to men. So full and complete was that revelation that Jesus could say "Anyone who has seen Me has seen the Father". He fully expresses the character of His Father; He is as Hebrews 1:3 has it, "The exact representation of His being". He consistently displayed love, faith and obedience. These are characteristics expected in Christian disciples, as discussed above. Moreover, just as to see Christ is to see the Father, so also to see the Christian should be to see Christ (1 Corinthians 11:1). The purpose of God in choosing disciples is that they should be conformed to the image of His Son (Romans 8:29); that is the full realization of their potential. If His character is to be seen in His disciples they must inevitably be engaged in doing His work.

Thus it is no surprise to hear Him say to Philip, "anyone who has faith in Me will do what I have been doing" and "even greater things" (which we judge to refer to the scope but not the nature or quality of the activities).

The Challenge to Disciples

PETER, THOMAS, PHILIP and the others in that Upper Room learned in those hours before Gethsemane, Gabbatha and Golgotha something of their role in the world for a Master in heaven and their potential in such service. The much-needed ministry seems to have been received with a slowness of perception that with our hindsight we too easily condemn. The Lord was explaining heavenly things to them and their earth-centred vision limited their appreciation of such truths. But Jesus reinforced His guidance with the simple statement that love to Him would result in obedience to His commands. Also the power of prayer was to be fully unleashed for them to use (for the Lord always gives the ability with the responsibility).

A further reinforcement was the promise to them of a place in the Father's house, which some commentators have understood to imply differing eternal stations for differing service here. In any event, the promise was one of proximity to the Lord forever. Our review of the character and potential of discipleship leaves us with inevitable questions in relation to our own service:

1. Is earthly preoccupation stunting our heavenly vision?

2. Are we quick to promise loyalty but slow to channel the love of Christ through ourselves to others?

3. Has the pattern and strength of our service been based on faith or human reasoning?

4. Have we, by our obedience to the teaching of Christ (which subsequently was called the apostles' teaching - Matthew 29:20; Acts 2:42) demonstrated our love to our Master?

5. As He continuously reviews our lives, does He see us ever growing more into conformity to the character He displayed?

Until the Lord takes us to the place where we belong, the character and potential of our discipleship should be seen, by the help of the Spirit, in our emulating the love, faith, obedience and other qualities we see in our Lord and Master.

CHAPTER SEVEN: THE PROMISE OF THE COMFORTER (GEORGE KENNEDY)

═══

One of the unsearchable beauties of the Lord is how He showed His love toward His disciples on that night when He was betrayed. "Having loved His own who were in the world, He loved them to the end" (John 13:1) and manifested that love in service, teaching and prayer. He who was soon to say, "My soul is exceeding sorrowful, even to death" (Matthew 26:38) and who Himself would be looking for comforters, but would find none (Psalm 69:20), spoke for the comfort of His eleven disciples, and for our comfort as well. The great Comforter spoke to them of another Comforter like Himself.

The Lord identified this Comforter (John 14:16) as the Spirit of truth (v.17), even the Holy Spirit (v.26). He is elsewhere called the Spirit of Christ (Romans 8:9; 1 Peter 1:11) who is now the believer's Advocate or Comforter with the Father (1 John 2:1). All such comfort and advocacy has strength because of truth and holiness. Much of this world's comfort is wishful thinking and sentimentality. Why? Because the world cannot receive the Comforter (v.17). The whole world lies in the evil one (1 John 5:19) in whom there is no truth, because he (Satan) is a liar and the father thereof (John 8:44). The child of God has a unique and blessed Person dwelling within, the Holy Spirit of God (Ephesians 4:30). We receive this Comforter when we receive the Lord Jesus as our personal Saviour (John 1:12; Ephesians 1:13).

The world, said the Lord, does not behold the Spirit of truth, neither does it know Him. The word "behold" is translated "perceive" in several places and "consider" in Hebrews 7:4; while the word "know" means to take in knowledge, to come to know, to recognize (W.E. Vine). For the Christian this wonderful Comforter is no unperceived Stranger but a Witness with our spirits that we are children of God and He is the Helper of our infirmity (Romans 8:16,26).

It should be evident that the Lord was promising His disciples another Person, not an influence nor an abstract, impersonal power. I have before me a letter from a Jehovah's Witness (so called) who writes - "Surely these instances speak of the Holy Spirit as a tool of God, rather than a being having its own initiative". Truly the world beholds Him not, neither knows Him. While it is true that the word "Spirit" (Greek: Theuma) is neuter gender in the original language, the Lord Jesus used the masculine personal pronoun seven times when speaking of the Holy Spirit.

The first occasion is in verse 26: "He shall teach you all things". The other occasions are John 15:26 ("He shall bear witness"), John 16:7 ("I will send Him unto you"), John 16:8 ("And He...will convict), John 16:13 ("When He ... is come" and "shall not speak from Himself"), and John 16:14 ("He shall glorify Me"). Usually the personal pronoun is implied by the form of the verb, but significantly the Lord uses a separate word for "He", specifying not only third person, but also masculine gender, to put the Personality of the Comforter beyond reach of doubt.

Four times the Lord spoke of the Holy Spirit as the Paraclete, and indeed He is the only One to do so. Literally it means "one called alongside", that is, to aid or help, to succour and to console, to plead another's cause. It is interesting to note that the Holy Spirit would be sent from alongside the Father (John 15:26). The Holy Spirit was already abiding (not "lives" as the NIV translates) alongside the disciples (John 14:17). The wonderful new reality was to be that the Holy Spirit would be "in you" and "with you forever". Never again would any child of God need to pray as David did, "do not take Your Holy Spirit from me" (Psalm 51:11). The indwelling Spirit brings great blessing, "the love of the Spirit" (Romans 15:30); and great responsibility: "do not grieve the Holy Spirit of God" (Ephesians 4:30).

In the New International Version the Greek word "parakletos" is translated "counsellor". Although "paraclete" could have a legal application, this did not apply to the Lord in His earthly ministry. When the Lord spoke of another Comforter, He was referring to One like Himself as He had been among them, and perhaps no more clearly seen than in that night before He died. Its general meaning is that of a Comforter or Helper, One who cheers on, encourages and exhorts. A legal connotation may be seen in 1 John 2:1. The work or service of the Paraclete is the Greek word "paraklesis" which is consistently expressed in the New Testament as comfort, consolation, exhortation and encouragement. In Acts 9:31 the early church is recorded as walking by the comfort (or exhortation) of the Holy Spirit coupled with the fear of the Lord. This is the secret of growth.

The Lord told the disciples that He would make request of the Father (not "pray"; the original word suggests equality and/or familiarity) for the gift of the Comforter (John 14:16). Martha had recently said to the Lord, "I know that, whatever You ask of God, God will give You" (John 11:22). Although she used the inappropriate word for "ask" in respect of the Lord's speaking to His Father, yet she knew with a perfectly accurate perception that God would grant His Son's request. If the disciples that night shared Martha's faith it must have been a great comfort to them when the Lord said that He would make request of the Father. The response would be assured. Thus, "the promise of My Father" is the promise to the Lord by the Father that He would send the Holy Spirit upon them (Luke 24:49; Acts 1:4). It was the Lord who received the promise of the Holy Spirit as Acts 2:33 makes clear and He poured forth Him whose power and presence were seen and heard on the day of Pentecost. The Paraclete is the Holy Spirit of promise by whom every believer is sealed (Ephesians 1:13) and we receive Him through faith (Galatians 3:14).

Concerning the coming of the Spirit of truth the Lord says, firstly, that the Father would give them another Comforter. He gives precedence to the Father. In the next reference He says that the Father would send the Holy Spirit in His name (John 14:26). Then in the third reference the Lord says that He will send the Comforter from the Father but also declares the Holy Spirit's activity, saying that He proceeds from the Father (John 15:26). Here is unity of purpose and action by the three Persons of the Godhead.

The Holy Spirit is God's gift, even as is His Son. Both were given, both sent forth (Galatians 4:4,6). Peter preached that his hearers would receive "The gift of the Holy Spirit" (Acts 2:38). "God...has given us His Holy Spirit" (1 Thessalonians 4:8) and through this gift God has shed abroad His love in our hearts (Romans 5:5). What a Comforter! "God has given us the Spirit in our hearts as a guarantee" (2 Corinthians 1:22; 5:5). The Holy Spirit has been "sent from heaven" (1 Peter 1:12) and yet He as the poet has said "has deigned to make His dwelling place these mortal bodies frail". He is indeed "a Guide, a Comforter bequeathed, with us to dwell".

In that solemn yet blessed night, the Lord spoke of the Comforter who was yet to come. That night is past as is the cross with its suffering and death. He is risen and exalted and glorified (see John 7:39), and we have received by faith (Galatians 3:2) the Spirit of adoption, whereby we cry, Abba, Father (Romans 8:15), having received, "not the spirit of the world, but the Spirit who is from God, that we might know the things that have been freely given to us by God." (1 Corinthians 2:12). How very much indeed He is the Paraclete - the Comforter!

CHAPTER EIGHT: THE VINE AND THE BRANCHES (ALAN SANDS)

─────

Have you ever been deceived by a bowl of plastic fruit? Perhaps you have at a distance; but you soon discovered that what was man-made, and very impressive, was only ornamental. It could do you no good. Only the real thing, the work of God, secured through human cooperation, can satisfy. This is the lesson of the Vine and its branches.

We are following in this book the very precious ministry given us by our Lord Jesus in the Upper Room within less than twenty-four hours of His cruel death for us at Calvary. John chapter fourteen closes with His words, "Arise, let us go from here". Knowing every detail of the horrors that lay before Him, He was ready to face all, yet such is His amazing grace, He was more concerned for our needs than for His own as He prepared to go out into that dreaded night. Marvellous Saviour!

The fruit of the vine was on the table. Possibly there was also a vine curled round the window or doorway visible to the disciples in the Upper Room. Obviously this could be no artificial plant - it would be real enough. Yet Jesus spoke of something even more real, more enduring. Though He would die the next day, He saw beyond Calvary to the fruitful relationship He would have with many: "I am the True Vine ... you are the branches" (vv. 1,5).

To the men gathered around the Lord that night, vines were most familiar. Their countryside was decked with them, and their Scriptures spoke often of them too. Fruitful vines symbolized all that was good and prosperous and joyful in God's original plan for His people, and their annual grape gathering was a happy period. But the Scriptures also used the vine to describe the sad failure of those same people: "Yet I had planted you a noble vine, a seed of highest quality. How then have you turned before Me Into the degenerate plant of an alien vine?" (Jeremiah 2:21).

How fitting that our Lord should take up the vine again, this time symbolic of a more wonderful divine plan; namely His own perfect self in unique and vital union with persons chosen and enabled to bear choice fruit to His Father's pleasure. The intimacy He thus describes is to be the very source of God-honouring happiness and effectiveness for the people of God today. From the metaphor of the vine and its branches our Lord vividly depicts the consistent outcome of true spiritual relationship with Him. Branches of the vine are exposed to the necessary light and atmosphere, but if cut off, they wither and die. Rather, they must feed on the hidden supply from the vine itself. What we call simply "sap" is a marvellous complex solution containing all the vital ingredients for life and healthy growth. So the branches just stay where they are and, tended by a careful vinedresser, take character from the vine and produce luscious clusters of grapes, bringing divinely intended benefit to others.

Now in the portion before us, the Lord uses the word "remain" (or "abide" as in the King James Version and Revised Version) no fewer than eleven times in the first ten verses, in contrast to His use of the word "go" just once in verse sixteen. Clearly He is stressing a most important principle, and we could express it paradoxically like this: THE SECRET OF SPIRITUAL PROGRESS IS TO STAY WHERE YOU ARE.

We who are described as "branches" are in Christ and, praise Him, we are eternally secure. However, our soul's security is not an issue in this discourse, but rather the effectiveness of our lives. They may be fruitful or fruitless; like branches laden with grapes, or sadly like withered twigs which God cannot use. The latter are so spiritually out of touch and useless as to be discarded like the dead branches on the fire. Whether this actually takes place during a lifetime or is the inevitable conclusion of the life reviewed at the judgement seat of Christ one cannot be dogmatic.

But on the positive side, both individually and collectively, real fulfilment and effectiveness in service will depend on our being careful to develop in our Christian experience our relationship with Christ. Our eternal souls are bound close to Him in love forever, and by faith and obedience our temporal lives can be lived in the joy of that closeness; bearing fruit and bringing glory to the Father (v.8). We may summarize what we are saying like this:

Union (In Christ) to Communion (With Christ) to Effective Service (Through Christ)

The order and frequency of the words "remain" and "go" are a challenge in themselves. Eleven times "remain" (representing communion) occurs before the one "go" (representing service). How disastrous when we put "go" first! Busy service without the energy and direction of prior communion will be rather like our bowl of plastic fruit -possibly impressive, but certainly useless.

How often one has been painfully reminded of our Lord's words on this occasion, "apart from Me you can do nothing" (v.5). Now we need men and women of action, "doers of the Word" in the best sense, and we should encourage as many as possible to get involved, but the ratio of "remain" to "go" is eleven-to-one. Surely we need to examine our lifestyle and ask ourselves the question, "Am I giving a high enough priority to remaining? Only to the extent that the branch is feeding will the fruit continue. Perhaps some of us need to spend more time in speaking to God, and less, but more effective time, in speaking to men.

In stressing this vital matter of our remaining, or abiding, in Him, our Lord brings before us in this passage seven essential elements which are as follows:

1. "He who abides in Me and I in him, bears much fruit" (v.5).

This practical fellowship with Christ entails a two-way commitment. He says, "Abide in Me, and I in you" (v.4 Revised Version). Clearly then if we are willing for Christ to take control in our lives He has promised to make them very fruitful.

2. "If you abide in Me, and My words abide in you "(v.7).

Reading, studying, memorizing, meditating in, and applying the Scriptures: all these are so important.

3. "Ask what you desire…whatever you ask the Father in My name He may give you" (vv.7,16).

What an encouragement to pray! Yet we have some difficulty with these words. Certainly, it is only as we allow His word to dominate our thoughts that His will becomes our wish (and daily cleansing will be a paramount wish of course).

4. "As the Father loved Me, I also have loved you; abide in My love" (v.9).

What boundless love! He laid down His life for us (v.13). This love seals our relationship with Him. How it should thrill our hearts! Now the enjoyment of His love, both to us, and through us, and the response of our own love to Him day-by-day require the yielding of our wayward will to Him, for we do not wish to grieve the One we love. He also says "Love one another as I have loved you" (v.12). So I cannot be truly abiding in Christ if I carry on just thinking about myself. May I then be increasingly concerned for others and enjoy their love in return.

5. "If you keep My commandments, you will abide in My love" (v.10).

So abiding in Christ not only involves hearing Him, speaking to Him, and thinking lovingly about Him, but it requires us to respond to His directions. Then the "going" we spoke of earlier is led by Him and is part of the experience of abiding in Him who said, "Go ... I am with you" (Matthew 28:19,20 Revised Version).

6. Every branch that does bear fruit He trims clean so that it "may bear more fruit" (v.2).

In ignorance one has stood aghast at the apparent drastic pruning by a skilled gardener. But the rich results which followed proved he knew what was best. So then, abiding in Christ will cause us to be properly sensitive to all God's dealings with us, and with His help we shall resist the temptation to complain or to become embittered. "No discipline seems pleasant at the time, but painful. Later on, however, it produces a harvest of righteousness and peace ("peaceable fruit" King James Version) for those who have been trained by it" (Hebrews 12:11).

7. "These things I have spoken to you, that My joy may remain in you" (v.11).

Although our Lord knew the great troubles which lay ahead, such was His devotion to God, He knew a unique calm and satisfaction. In contrast, we don't know what lies ahead; but He speaks these words to us so that though we may be baffled at times, we can be strengthened by the serenity which comes with His own dear presence, and our submitting to His own perfect will.

Finally, regarding the fruit itself (the mark of true disciples - v.8), we may be sure that if we attend to the abiding, God will attend to His fruit. It will manifest itself in such things as:

1. WHOLENESS - The development of a balanced Christ-like character with those precious inward and outward graces, "the fruit of the Spirit" (Galatians 5:22-23).

2. WORSHIP - "The fruit of lips" confessing His glorious name (Hebrews 13:15).

3. WITNESS - The manner of life "bearing fruit in every good work" (Colossians 1:10).

4. WINNING - The vital "spiritual reproduction" through leading another to Christ. Though we may be deeply conscious of past failure, may we be encouraged by our Lord's words: "I chose ... that you should go and bear fruit ... and that your fruit should remain" (v.16).

Ours are peace and joy divine

Who are one with Christ,

When, like branches in the vine,

We abide in Christ.

As a living grafted shoot,

Nourished from a hidden root,

We may bear all holy fruit

Through the love of Christ.

Love of Christ!

Clusters grow on every branch,

Through the love of Christ.

CHAPTER NINE: THE DISCIPLE AND THE WORLD (LEN SHATTOCK)

═══

The little band of men upon whom the Lord would centre His commission to disciple the nations were left in no doubt at all by His words to them that they would be His witnesses in the face of human hostility. He therefore urged them to bind themselves together in the strength of their love one for another and in that strength face the hatred of the world. The keynote in His statement to them is "A servant is not greater than his Master" (John 15:20). It is inevitable that as the world persecuted and rejected the Son of God so it will persecute and reject those who follow and faithfully represent Him. The call of the Lord Jesus to discipleship brings separation from a world in opposition to God and His Christ.

That distinction, when manifestly expressed, invokes the antagonism of unregenerate society, for the world loves its own and hates that which is not of itself and of its own nature.

This world has known the presence of the incarnate Son of God and the revelation of divine truth which He brought into it, and the wonder of divine grace which prompted Him to redeem sinners by dying an atoning death on their behalf. The condemnation of the world is in its rejection of the Christ, a fact underscored by His own words, "If I had not come and spoken to them, they would have no sin: but now they have no excuse for their sin" (John 15:22).

The tragedy of human existence without God is that it is enslaved and dominated by devastating forces of wickedness. Behind all man's rejection of God and Christ and of the revealed truth of Scripture, and the principles of holiness which govern life related to God, are Satan and the spiritual hosts of evil which he directs. As such the Devil is identified by the Lord Jesus as "the prince of this world" (John 12:31; John 14:30; John 16:11). The Scriptures describe him as "the spirit who now works in the sons of disobedience" (Ephesians 2:2) and also as "the god of this age (who) has blinded, (those) who do not believe" (2 Corinthians 4:4). The spiritual hosts of wickedness which the Devil commands are described as "the rulers of the darkness of this age" (Ephesians 6:12).

The graphic phrase "the darkness" is the Holy Spirit's diagnosis of world condition spiritually. As it was in the days of the apostle, so now, it is an equally accurate description of human life under the destructive power of spiritual evil. The age in which we live supplies multiplying evidence of the darkness which engulfs mankind. Salacious writings which most people would have been ashamed to have on their bookshelves are now popularly acclaimed as being of literary worth. What might have been alleged to be subtle in media presentation of deviant behaviour is now blatantly portrayed, and exists as a terrifying incitement to impurity.

Against such streams of corruption the disciple faces the challenge of the Lord's words "You are the salt of the earth" (Matthew 5:13). Salt is antiseptic, astringent, arresting corruption. This influence in Christian witness is an essential part of the divine intention affecting discipleship. How tragic "if the salt loses its flavour"! Flavourless salt is no longer salt. If a believer in Christ conforms to the spirit of the age in which he lives, his Christian identity is lost, his discipleship destroyed and his testimony nullified. There is always the need for vigilance to obey the command "Do not love the world, or the things in the world" (1 John 2:15). Failure in this deflected Demas from discipleship (2 Timothy 4:10) as it has diverted from the same pathway his successors in the same failure.

In every sphere of living of the Christian disciple, priority of claim belongs to the Lord Jesus. The terms of his following His master are not negotiable. As they are outlined in Luke 14 they seem severe and hard to understand. "If anyone comes to Me and does not hate his father and mother, wife and children, brothers and sisters, yes, and his own life also, he cannot be My disciple." (Luke 14:26). These words must not be construed as meaning that obedient disciples must adopt a malevolent attitude toward their loved ones - this would contradict such scriptures as Ephesians 5:25. What they define is an attitude which makes the claims of the Lord Jesus supreme above all other relationships. In fact such claims are to be superior to every demand of the self-life (Luke 14:27). In the face of the rampant greed surrounding him in a godless world, the disciple is called to renounce all that he has (Luke 14:33).

In effect this means that he must not be held back from following the Lord by the claims of others or by that which he himself possesses. From such claims we may instinctively recoil until we understand why they are so imperative to discipleship. The teaching of the Lord Jesus is not for mere academic debate or to satisfy intellectual curiosity. It demands obedience, and when obeyed emancipates us from every ensnaring entanglement which impedes our following Him. "If you abide in My word, you are My disciples indeed. And you shall know the truth, and the truth shall make you free" (John 8:31-32). The freedom which He brings us, as we abide in His word and are truly His disciples, is from every false concept which distorts the outlook of an unbelieving world. It frees us also from every ecclesiastical error which false interpretation of Scripture has imposed upon the minds of men, and in that freedom establishes us to witness faithfully to the truth which is revealed through Him.

Although living in a world of people who by nature are "alienated from the life of God" (Ephesians 4:19) the Christian is called to live a holy life. He is to "put away" all that which characterized his living before Christ saved him (see Ephesians 4:22-24). The grace of God has taught him to deny (that is to say "NO" to) ungodly lusts and to live soberly and righteously in this present world (Titus 2:11-14). Such a pattern of life will demonstrate that he is among the company of the redeemed to whom God's power has granted "all things that pertain to life and godliness, through the knowledge of Him who called us by glory and virtue ... having escaped the corruption that is in the world through lust" (2 Peter 1:3-4).

The Lord told His own "If they persecuted Me, they will also persecute you". Holiness ever condemns corruption; obedience is a constant rebuke to rebellion. In describing the witness of His own the Lord said, "You are the light of the world" (Matthew 5:14). Light is an irritant to men who love darkness rather than the light because their deeds are evil. For, in Scripture, "light" often means "truth and knowledge" and conversely "darkness" implies "error and ignorance".

To live a life in which the claims of Christ are supreme means that inevitably the disciple will face the ridicule and contempt of a society dominated by godless materialism. Often he will be misunderstood by his unsaved kinsfolk. In the fiercest expression of opposition he will face persecution from a world inflamed by hatred of the Lord Jesus. The Master tells us "All these things they will do to you for My Name's sake" (John 15:21).

"For My Name's sake". This is the motivation which impels disciples to truly represent their Lord despite the opposing forces arrayed against them. Yet He has revealed that such witness to Himself will be a double witness. It will be the witness of the Spirit and also that of His own (John 15:26-27). In the energy of the Holy Spirit that is the only witness in this world capable of bringing conviction to men and women, boys and girls, whose minds are by nature at enmity with God.

Even as the Lord predicted, the days of persecution dawned for those first century disciples (e.g. Acts 8:1). Their faithful witness aroused the opposition of Jewish rulers, of pagan Gentiles and of Roman Caesars.

The Lord had told them, "the time is coming that whoever kills you will think that he offers God service." (John 16:2). An outstanding illustration of this was Saul of Tarsus (Acts 26:9). Yet divine grace changed the persecutor into the preacher of the gospel and to being Paul the apostle of Jesus Christ who urged the Philippian saints to be "blameless and harmless, children of God without fault in the midst of a crooked and perverse generation, among whom you shine as lights in the world, holding fast the word of life" (Philippians 2:15-16).

Today, in the western world, Christian disciples live comparatively comfortable lives. By no stretch of the imagination can the ridicule we may sometimes experience be called persecution. Yet, even now, there are countries where God-denying political dogmas cause governments to inflict harsh punishment upon those who faithfully witness to the Lord Jesus. We should be constantly praying for these our brethren and sisters in Christ, and be thanking God that in the face of such oppression faithful witness to Himself is still maintained. Meanwhile, for us all, the claims of discipleship remain relevant; they are unchanged and undiminished. Let us awake from mediocrity in spiritual living by obediently answering them as those committed to the cause of the Master.

World trends in mounting opposition to God imply that the Lord may be telling us "the hour is coming" and we shall be required to face an experience which will prove that "all who desire to live godly in Christ Jesus will suffer persecution" (2 Timothy 3:12). Should this ever be - may we seek now the grace which will find us with those "counted worthy to suffer shame for His name" (Acts 5:41).

CHAPTER TEN: THE HOLY SPIRIT'S MINISTRY (JOHN ARCHIBALD)

T he Lord knew everything about His disciples. Time after time they found that their very thoughts were known to Him. On the last night before Calvary the Lord from heaven spoke to His apostles of many things, and even as He spoke He understood the effect of His words well.

He knew that their hearts were filled with sorrow at the prospect of His departure from them. He had filled their hearts and their lives in such a blessed way that the thought of being without Him was utterly devastating. But their sorrow was great because they did not yet understand where He was going. None of them asked Him. If those disciples had appreciated the triumph and the glory of the return to heaven of the mighty Victor of Calvary, and if they had grasped the full weight of His promise, "I go to prepare a place for you" (John 14:2) then surely their thoughts would have been very different. However, the gracious Master faithfully told them the truth although He well understood the disciples' limited ability to absorb it.

It is against this background of perplexity and sadness of heart that the Lord gives them the promise "If I go, I will send Him to you" (v.7). This happy assurance stands in splendour alongside His earlier word, "if I go and prepare a place for you, I will come again and receive you to Myself" (John 14:3). Not only were they promised His personal return but in His absence they were to have the constant presence of the Comforter. No wonder Paul describes Him as the Holy Spirit of promise in Ephesians 1:13. Not only did the Comforter come in blessed fulfilment of the promise given, but His ministry and His very presence are a real and present pledge of that great promise yet to be fulfilled,

"I will come again and receive you to Myself". Now in the portion we are considering, before the Lord speaks of the Spirit's ministry to the believer, He first refers to:

The Holy Spirit and The World

IT IS THE SPIRIT'S work to convict or reprove the world and in doing so He inevitably establishes the attitude that the disciple ought to have towards it. This is clearly stated by Paul, "the world has been crucified to me, and I to the world" (Galatians 6:14) and by John, "Do not love the world, or the things in the world" (1 John 2:15). Three subjects form the basis of the Holy Spirit's convicting of the world, and they must be the starting point in any awakening of sinful man to the true knowledge of God.

The first is sin. Sin is universal in the world since all have sinned. It stands between God and men as a mighty barrier which is far beyond human ability to remove - So great is its power that its victims are unaware of its full gravity and seriousness. The world of mankind does not recognize its desperate guilt before God. Just as the Lord Jesus denounced sin in uncompromising terms, so does the Spirit of God. The world is a world of unbelief in Christ and no one in it could begin to appreciate how hopeless is their case without the blessed ministry of the Spirit.

The second subject is righteousness and this is linked with the departure of Christ to the Father and His absence from the world. In the world of men "there is none righteous, no, not one". The Lord Jesus is the only perfectly righteous man who has ever walked this earth. When He was here His words and His conduct shone in brilliant splendour against the murky background of the corrupt ways and institutions of men. What an experience for those who companied with Him during His short time here! They had first-hand knowledge of the searching brightness of His divine character and some even turned away from the brightness. This declaring of the divine standard is continued by the Holy Spirit, who not only reproves sin but also declares absolute righteousness in a world without Christ.

Thirdly, judgement - and here the Lord refers to the alien prince of a world which is alienated from God and His Christ. John says elsewhere, "the whole world lies under the sway of the evil one" (1 John 5:19). It is the mighty Adversary of God and men who has blinded the minds of the unbelieving. But the divine sentence of judgement has already been pronounced on that evil prince, and judgement will pass to all who remain deceived by him. The godless society of men is doomed and it is the Spirit's work to make this clear. If anyone from such a world would find the way back to God then the way must begin with a deep awareness of sin, an understanding of the perfect righteousness of God as displayed so marvellously in Christ, and a lively recognition that mankind is under sentence of eternal judgement. Thank God for the gracious presence in the world of the Comforter, without whose helpful ministry none could ever escape.

The Holy Spirit and The Believer

HAVING CONSIDERED THE threefold ministry of the Spirit in the world, we review now His threefold ministry in the experience of the disciple of the Lord. We learn that "He will guide you into all truth" (John 16:13). Then "He shall declare unto you the things that are to come" (v.13), and thirdly "He will glorify Me" (John 16:14).

In the first of these promises the spirit is given the title Spirit of Truth. Now truth can be an uncomfortable thing. God's ways are not our ways and His plan for us will often contain elements that surprise us and which may not conform to our ideas of rightness. If we are to have our grasp of divine truth enlarged then we need to expect that our ideas will need adjustment and we shall need a powerful guide. But in the end, the greater our appreciation the greater will be our joy. We have noted already that as the disciples began to understand that their Lord was going away, their hearts were filled with sorrow. As their understanding increased to take in the triumph of His resurrection and the glory of His exaltation to heaven's throne and the promise of His coming again, their sorrow gave place to joy and their witness acquired an irresistible momentum.

So it is for His disciples today. It is the Lord's desire that we should not settle for a limited appreciation of His truth, resting on a comfortable understanding and afraid to follow the Spirit's prompting to move forward. We have His promise, "He will guide you into all truth". With such a guide there is nothing to fear. Without Him we shall find only error.

Second is the promise that He shall declare unto you the things that are to come. This should be seen in the light of verse 4: "But these things I have told you, that when the time comes, you may remember that I told you of them." The Lord emphasizes that "He will not speak on His own authority, but whatever He hears He will speak". The Spirit's ministry forms a unity with the teaching of the Lord. It is nowhere at variance with the Lord's words and its content does not extend beyond what the Lord has said. This is an important point on which some have sadly erred. The sweet promise is, that whatever the future holds for the disciple of the Lord, the ministry of the Spirit will be more than sufficient to equip the disciple to face it. In the most difficult times the Comforter will help our understanding and will strengthen us to accept the will of the Lord, even when we cannot understand. He knows the end from the beginning.

Thirdly, "He will glorify Me, for He will take of what is Mine and declare it to you". Here we have God the Spirit glorifying God the Son. In the following chapter the Lord speaks of the Father glorifying the Son and of the Son glorifying the Father. It is a sublime contemplation that the Persons of Deity should glorify one another. The glory of God can be thought of as the effect on the beholder of God's greatness. It is therefore a great privilege for a man to glorify God. It means that the greatness of God has so affected the man as to produce in him attitudes and actions which reflect that divine greatness.

Now think of this applied to the Persons of Deity. In this case the Holy Spirit so appreciates the Person of the Son that He, the Spirit, reflects and declares the greatness of the Son. The theme of the Spirit's ministry is therefore Christ the Son of God. There could be no greater help and comfort than this. For those disciples to whom the Lord spoke in our chapter, there stretched out the prospect of days and weeks and years of their Master's absence. They had been enriched beyond telling by His company with them day by day since the unforgettable day that they first met Him and decided to become disciples. To them He gives the promise that God the Spirit will come and abide in them and day by day increase their store of the unsearchable riches of Christ.

Along with these promises there comes a reminder of who He is who makes the promise. "All things that the Father has are Mine." In the presence of those first disciples was the Man of Galilee who seemed to have no earthly power or wealth. In fact all things belong to Him and all things were made by Him. Can it be that He is saying that all the power and resource of Deity is there to be taken and made known to the disciple for his help? Yes indeed, but only through the agency of the Spirit of truth.

And every virtue we possess,

And every victory won,

And every thought of holiness,

Are His alone.

CHAPTER ELEVEN: THE FATHER HIMSELF LOVES YOU (BRIAN FULLARTON)

———

A part from and before all created existence is the infinite and holy fellowship of the three Persons of the Godhead. Although one God, indivisible in essence, Father, Son and Spirit are distinguishable in personality and distinctive in functions within the Godhead. There is a relationship of infinite love and joy between Father, Son and Holy Spirit.

Eternal Love and the Triune God

"THE FATHER LOVES ME" (John 10:17 Revised Standard Version). The Son of God was the worthy and adequate object of the Father's love when on earth and the One for whose glory the Spirit labours now. The Father's love and delight in the Son, however, was not confined to His life on earth, it existed before the foundation of the world (John 17:24). The Father is the source of all blessing for us, the Son has brought the blessing to us and the Holy Spirit makes good the blessing in us. The Father's love is the fount of all His giving, a love that lavishes its fullness upon its object.

God is self-sufficient. But His eternal love must find expression. "God is love" (1 John 4:8); love is not an attribute, but His very nature. It is described in Ephesians 2:4 as "His great love", unchanging, unending, incomprehensible. One beautiful implication of the unity of divine Persons is the existence of the sublimest fellowship of infinite love without a shadow of incompatibility, the most exquisite accord and most perfect unity and oneness of mind. Heaven is resplendent with the expression of this concept of highest fellowship. But eternal love embraces and draws others into that circle of sweetest communion - "God of all the families of Israel ... with lovingkindness I have drawn you." (Jeremiah 31:1,3).

So, "the Father loves you" comes to us as disciples in a warmth of love which may bring ceaseless enjoyment as we ponder its eternal wealth and vast purposes of blessing. The apostle John refers to the Father's love as being of a singular quality. What belongs to heaven is totally different from anything associated with the world's concept of love - "what manner of (Greek: potapos - what sort or kind) love the Father has bestowed ..." (1 John 3:1). This love produces astonishment, admiration and, above all, adoration in its beneficiaries. It exceeds all other love in its magnitude (Ephesians 2:4); it defies explanation (Ephesians 3:19) and description (1 John 3:1). Its contemplation leads the believer in the Lord Jesus to sever himself from likeness to the world and become conformed to the likeness of the Son of God. Divine love was the moving force in redemption's plan; love that is more than sentiment, it reveals itself in action.

The Title of "Father"

THE OPENING SENTENCE of Hebrews chapter 1 tells us that God has fully and finally spoken in One who is Son, inferring the corresponding revelation of God the Father. This was the title constantly on the lips of the Lord Jesus. Six times in John 17 the Lord mentions "Father" in prayer, so in manifesting God's Name (v.6) there is no doubt what that Name is. "Show us the Father" said Philip; all that a child of God needs is to know God as "the Father" with all that this title implies. The God of the Bible is no nameless, faceless force, only to be feared and placated. He delights to express His infinity in terms which the Spirit-enlightened person can understand and glorify His Name. He is faithful, capable, strong, forgiving, tender and compassionate. The heaven of heavens cannot contain Him yet He is pleased to take up loving abode with those who know the Son.

The distinctive title of God in the New Testament is "Father" (Greek: pater). Old Testament variations of this usage are seen in such scriptures as Isaiah 63:16 in the nation of Israel's seeking forgiveness and restoration: "You, O LORD, are our Father". At the time of Malachi the priests who, with national pride, referred to Jehovah as Father, in reality had been despising His Name by their conduct. The Name of God represents His identity, authority, personality, character, rank, majesty, power and excellence.

Abba, Father

A CAREFUL READING OF the contexts where the words "ABBA, FATHER" are found - Mark 14:36, Romans 8:15 and Galatians 4:6 - show that this expression is not a "baby cry" but the name given to the Father by a mature son. "Father" itself implies family relationship, but while in infancy there is delight in the simplicity of the bond, in maturing years the title conveys the thought of sonship with truc values and corresponding responsibilities. "Abba" is Aramaic, a word associated with the older Hebrew word "AB" meaning "Father". The root of the noun comprises two Hebrew characters - ALEPH (first, preeminent) and BETH (in, inside, particularly of a house). The thought is that of filial obedience. The Father has life in Himself, sustains and tutors His own, making every provision for their welfare. He meets every need. In the Lord's form of address in Mark 14, there is the recognition of need, acknowledgment of the Father's power and submission to His Father's will. No rhetoric can rise to the appeal of the heart-expression "Abba, Father".

The relationship between God as Father and His children is spiritual, established by grace on His part and the response of faith on theirs.

By faith in the Son of God we know God as Father in the affectionate intimacy of His family "circle" (John 1:12).

Sons of God

IN SPEAKING TO GOD as "Father" the Spirit of God confirms to our human spirit the truth of family-ship - we are children of God (Romans 8:15,16). Grandiose forms of addressing God are superfluous. His delight is to hear His children call Him "Father". He hears no more than what the heart speaks. Through faith in Christ Jesus we are sons of God, sons of a heavenly Father (Galatians 3:26; Matthew 6:6). In the latter verse the emphasis is on the child's trust and dependence; in the former, the status is given through the operation of the faith-principle. The Sonship of the Lord Jesus is absolutely unique and independent of those who exercise faith. He is the only-begotten Son. He is "The Son", we are "sons". "Because you are sons, God has sent forth the Spirit of His Son into your hearts" (Galatians 4:6).

Although the Lord taught the disciples to pray "Our Father", He never used this expression. The Sonship of Christ is His own unique glory as co-equal, co-existent and co-eternal with the Father, dwelling in the perfect intimacy of the Godhead and, above all, as being the supreme object of the Father's love. Time never was, nor can be, when the Son is other than the joy of the Father's heart and the light of the Father's face. The Son has met with complete response every desire of the heart of His God.

The spontaneous invocation of God as "The God and Father of our Lord Jesus Christ" is evidenced by obedience (1 Peter 1:3). That is a token of the indwelling Spirit's power in the life of the saint who gives acknowledgment of Jesus as his Lord. The evidence of love is obedience; to withhold obedience is a practical denial of the lordship and authority of Christ. True love in the disciple's heart yields glad obedience which is not slavish observance to a rigid law to which penalties are attached. In Scripture the title "sons of God" so often conveys and emphasizes the high dignity of fellowship with God through obedience to His will, rather than simply the possession of the divine life by new birth. In John 4:23 the Lord Jesus speaks of those who "worship the Father". This is worship based on a relationship of obedience and love to God as "The Father" in "spirit and truth"; such does "the Father" seek to be His worshippers.

By receiving Christ we become children of God (John 1:12); by obedience to Christ and in fellowship with Him the Father receives us as sons and daughters (2 Corinthians 6:15, 17-18). The Father's heart responds to every circumstance of His people, the faintest throb of the saints' hearts finds a counterpart in that great, divine heart of love. Love in the heart of a weak friend mocks by its futility to help; love in the Father's heart imparts power, joy and peace.

Providential Care of Fatherhood

THE LORD APPEALED IN Matthew 7:9-11 to the natural care of imperfect fatherhood as an argument for confidence in the greater, perfect care of a heavenly Father. Natural love in a father, while sincere, is never perfect; moreover, human wisdom is limited, and what appears to be beneficial in the natural realm might turn out to be harmful. The Father's love is measured by His love for the Son. It is the love of God in Christ Jesus our Lord from which no power on earth or heaven can separate us (Romans 8:39).

Knowing the Father's love is no guarantee of immunity from difficulties and trials. A natural father knows it is not in the best interests of his child to shelter him from every difficulty and disappointment. There is a learning process through difficulties and problems that gives fitness for adult life. The chief concern of our Father is the development of

Christlikeness in character which helps in understanding much that would otherwise be inexplicable in spiritual experience. He desires fitness and capability for this life in which there is training for responsibilities and privileges in the life to come. The Lord Jesus, as in all else, gave the perfect example of confidence in His Father when, from a human standpoint, all had seemed to go awry - "... for so it seemed good in Your sight" (Matthew 11:20-26).

Praise our God who willed it thus,

Praise His Son who died for us,

Praise the Father for the Son,

Who so vast a work hath done.

CHAPTER TWELVE: FINAL SUPPLICATIONS (JACK FERGUSON)

———

The Background to John 17

The Lord Jesus was still in the Upper Room, alone with the Eleven. Judas had gone out to finalize the betrayal. It was night. But there was no darkness in the Room; just joy and serenity radiating from the Son of the Father's love, as He thought of the glory of the finished work, and Home, and of the Father's care for those He would leave behind. He had communed for the last time with His disciples. Now He would audibly, in their presence, commend them to His Father and the Eleven would hear the confirmation of His promises to them.

He prayed in two different places that night. The Synoptic gospels record tenderly the garden prayer of Jesus, the Son of Mary. That was an agony prayer, anticipating Calvary and dereliction. But with John it was typically different. He records what was designated by a sixteenth-century theologian as "the high-priestly prayer" of the Son of God, thoughtful as to the needs of His followers, calm in His own majestic place in the Father's sovereignty.

Verses 1 - 5

IN HIS SUBLIME OPENING meditation the Lord Jesus revealed that in His mind, as the eternal Son, His mission on earth was now complete. The "hour" had come at last. It had not come in John 7:30; was on its way in 12:23; now it would be on the morrow. It was the hour of Calvary. It was the final glory of submission to the Father's will. Through this act of obedience, the Father would be eternally glorified and by means of it the Son would grant eternal life to all those whom the Father would give Him. In the temple of His body He had expressed the Father's glory; the work for which He was commissioned had been accomplished; now He longed for the Father to glorify Him alongside Himself with the glory they had shared before the world was. Truly our spirits worship before such fulfilments of eternal forethought.

Verses 6 - 10

ISRAEL HAD ENJOYED majestic names of God. Hebrew expressions in the several forms of El, Jah, Adon; names such as Shaddai; or the various combinations of the divine name such as Adonai Jehovah; these were all rich revelations of God in His power, lordship and covenant relationship. But the references to Father in the Old Testament had been few. Its full revelation in all its affection was reserved for the day when the eternal Son came in human gentleness. He had revealed it to the men and women (Greek: anthropoi) God had given Him; but in particular to the eleven men with Him in the Room; men of Israel given by the Father to the Son.

They had been His own little fellowship of companions in His experiences. To these He had given the Father's new teaching. They had found it hard at times to receive - but they loyally accepted His deity and held on when others turned back. It was these men, not Israel or the world generally, who were the subject of His prayer. Everything was going to depend on them; and in them by the Spirit's help His confidence would be justified. "I am glorified in them". Such was the appreciation of the One who alone could say by reason of His deity, "All Mine are Yours, and Yours are Mine".

Verses 11 - 16

AT THIS POINT, THE main burden of the Lord's intercession was revealed. During the period of His ministry, He had been central to the little group. He had held them together when their different personalities and backgrounds might have made for division. He had taught them the balanced way of enjoying victory and accepting defeat. He had demonstrated the life of suffering for righteousness' sake and shown them the path of greatness in His kingdom. He had alerted them to the weakness of self and the power of the Spirit. He had both watched over them and protected them so that the enemy had only been able to destroy the life of the twelfth man. He had kept them safe in the Father's name.

But now He was going Home, leaving them to face a hostile world which would hate them because His word had made them strangers to it. Henceforth their safety from the evil one would lie in their own maintenance of harmony in unity. For this His word, His joy, His intercession were vital. He had earlier referred to "Father" in relation to Himself. Now He referred to "Holy Father" regarding the sanctification of His own men. He made specific request, "Holy Father, keep through Your name those whom You have given Me, that they may be one as We are."

Verses 17 - 23

NOR WAS IT SIMPLY A matter of leaving the Eleven behind. These were the men to whom He had purposely given the Father's word. They had been His men in training. Now they would become His front-line men, sent with a sacred commitment into the world, just as the Father had initially sent Him. Under the Spirit's guidance they would oversee the spread of His word to the nations. Only men specifically set apart in the truth of the Father's word could undertake such a task. Not only so, but only those kept together in the same harmony of unity could in due course have fellowship with them, take over from them and continue the same truth of God down the centuries.

So for this He prayed and again the same burden is revealed: "That they all may be one" (v.21); "that they also may be one" (v.22); "that they may be made perfect in one" (v.23). And it was all for the purpose "that the world may know that You have sent Me, and have loved them as You have loved Me" (v.23). Thus He pleaded with His Father for a unity among His followers which the world would both see and know. A unity visible in operation, tangible, recognizable, corporate. Not surely the unity of the Church the Body, for that Church is necessarily one in a unity which requires no prayerful protection from 'the gates of Hades". Rather it must have been the unity of the churches of God into which the Eleven were shortly to be called, together with those who would similarly be prepared to be set apart in the truth of the Father's word.

Through that word of truth they would become "perfect in one". There was a sense of consummation of purpose in the word "perfect". The formation of the churches of God in the post-Pentecost period would be the completion of the purposes of God in testimony for this dispensation. As a result of the Atonement, believing sinners would become members of the Church the Body, with eternal security. They would then be called upon to be baptized as disciples, added to churches of God, and there give individual and collective effect to the whole counsel of God. There they would be perfected into a corporate unity, and from one point of view the purpose of God in their life would be complete.

It would need the Father's help and the cooperation of willing hearts to maintain the harmony in unity of that testimony. Yet only by this means would the world effectively see and know the reality of the Father's love.

Verses 24 - 26

BUT HE HAD USED THE word "may". He knew that He prayed for a unity among His followers which the enemy, perhaps above all else, would attack. The Trinity was united in giving all for it, was so deserving of it, yet would sorrowfully see it fragmented as time went on. Now the Intercessor "willed" a request in these final verses which the Father will grant one day. As He sat in the Room that night there was no evidence of glory; just the well-loved Master in the simple, home-spun robe, weary from a long day, filled with the sorrow of oncoming betrayal, denial and abandonment. Yet these eleven men had left all in faith to follow Him, won by His love, persuaded as to the ultimate triumph of His cause - how He loved them for it!

So He asked His Father that one day they too might come Home and see His glory, which like the Father's love, He had known before the foundation of the world. The world of men didn't understand. Had they recognized the "Righteous Father" in the Son, they would not be crucifying Him the following day. But He had told the Eleven of the Father's love and they had believed it. Henceforth, He would rely on them to spearhead the spread of the tidings of the significance of the Father's name, of the reality of the Father's love.

And as He interceded that night in the Room for His own, so we believe that today, almost two thousand years later, He still pleads for His followers as He ministers in the heavenly sanctuary. Gladly He must have seen the vast spread of the knowledge of the Father's love. Sadly He must observe that it has not been in the harmony of unity of the Father's word. The words of His prayer are bound to affect our spirits. He would still have us all to be "made perfect into one". That, we submit, is the unity which is presented in the New Testament as a unity beyond the unity of the Church the Body. It is the perfecting of disciples into corporate unity in testimony in the fellowship of churches of God. It is maintained by the principle of rule in the kingdom of God under the guidance of the Spirit in a united elderhood. May the Lord help us not to fail Him in this.

Did you love *In the Shadow of Calvary: A Bible Study of John 12-17*?
Then you should read *8 Amazing Privileges of God's People: A Bible
Study of Romans 9:4-5* by Brian Johnston!

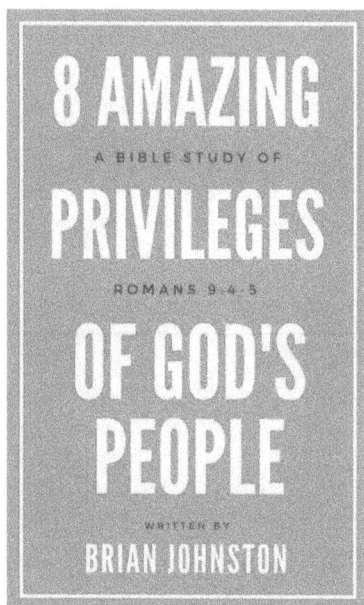

8 AMAZING
A BIBLE STUDY OF
PRIVILEGES
ROMANS 9:4-5
OF GOD'S
PEOPLE
WRITTEN BY
BRIAN JOHNSTON

The apostle Paul says in Romans 9:4-5: "who are Israelites, to whom
pertain the adoption, the glory, the covenants, the giving of the law, the
service of God, and the promises; of whom are the fathers and from
whom, according to the flesh, Christ came, who is over all, the eternally
blessed God, Amen."

Perhaps you hadn't noticed this little gem tucked away in the middle
of the letter, but it is a tremendous description of what it meant to be
among God's people in the past. We are not so much interested in a
history lesson, of course, but in seeing to what extent each of these eight
great can find its answer today in our service for God.

Also by Hayes Press

Bible Studies
Bible Studies 1990 - First Samuel
Bible Studies 1991 - The First Letter of Paul to the Corinthians
Bible Studies 1993 - Second Samuel
Bible Studies 1994 - The Establishment and Development of Churches of God
Bible Studies 1995 - The Kings of Judah and Israel from Solomon to Asa
Bible Studies 1992 - The Second Letter of Paul to the Corinthians

Needed Truth
Needed Truth 1888
Needed Truth 2001
Needed Truth 2002
Needed Truth 2003
Needed Truth 2004
Needed Truth 2005
Needed Truth 2006
Needed Truth 2007
Needed Truth 2008
Needed Truth 2009
Needed Truth 2010

Needed Truth 2011
Needed Truth 2012
Needed Truth 2015
Needed Truth 1888-1988: A Centenary Review of Major Themes

Standalone
The Road Through Calvary: 40 Devotional Readings
Lovers of God's House
Different Discipleship: Jesus' Sermon on the Mount
The House of God: Past, Present and Future
The Kingdom of God
Knowing God: His Names and Nature
Churches of God: Their Biblical Constitution and Functions
Four Books About Jesus
Collected Writings On ... Exploring Biblical Fellowship
Collected Writings On ... Exploring Biblical Hope
Collected Writings On ... The Cross of Christ
Builders for God
Collected Writings On ... Exploring Biblical Faithfulness
Collected Writings On ... Exploring Biblical Joy
Possessing the Land: Spiritual Lessons from Joshua
Collected Writings On ... Exploring Biblical Holiness
Collected Writings On ... Exploring Biblical Faith
Collected Writings On ... Exploring Biblical Love
These Three Remain...Exploring Biblical Faith, Hope and Love
The Teaching and Testimony of the Apostles
Pressure Points - Biblical Advice for 20 of Life's Biggest Challenges
More Than a Saviour: Exploring the Person and Work of Jesus
The Psalms: Volumes 1-4 Boxset
The Faith: Outlines of Scripture Doctrine
Key Doctrines of the Christian Gospel

Is There a Purpose to Life?
Bible Covenants 101
The Hidden Christ - Volume 2: Types and Shadows in Offerings and Sacrifices
The Hidden Christ Volume 1: Types and Shadows in the Old Testament
The Hidden Christ - Volume 3: Types and Shadows in Genesis
Heavenly Meanings - The Parables of Jesus
Fisherman to Follower: The Life and Teaching of Simon Peter
Called to Serve: Lessons from the Levites
Needed Truth 2017 Issue 1
The Breaking of the Bread: Its History, Its Observance, Its Meaning
Spiritual Revivals of the Bible
An Introduction to the Book of Hebrews
The Holy Spirit and the Believer
The Psalms: Volume 1 - Thoughts on Key Themes
The Psalms: Volume 2 - Exploring Key Elements
The Psalms: Volume 3 - Surveying Key Sections
The Psalms: Volume 4 - Savouring Choice Selections
Profiles of the Prophets
The Hidden Christ - Volumes 1-4 Box Set
The Hidden Christ - Volume 4: Types and Shadows in Israel's Tabernacle
Baptism - Its Meaning and Teaching
Conflict and Controversy in the Church of God in Corinth
In the Shadow of Calvary: A Bible Study of John 12-17
Moses: God's Deliverer
Sparkling Facets: Bible Names and Titles of Jesus
A Little Book About Being Christlike
Keys to Church Growth
From Shepherd Boy to Sovereign: The Life of David
Back to Basics: A Guide to Essential Bible Teaching
An Introduction to the Holy Spirit

Israel and the Church in Bible Prophecy
"Growth and Fruit" and Other Writings by John Drain
15 Hot Topics For Today's Christian
Needed Truth Volume 2 1889
Studies on the Return of Christ
Studies on the Resurrection of Christ
Needed Truth Volume 3 1890
The Nations of the Old Testament: Their Relationship with Israel and Bible Prophecy
The Message of the Minor Prophets
Insights from Isaiah
The Bible - Its Inspiration and Authority
Lessons from Ezra and Nehemiah
A Bible Study of God's Names For His People
Moses in One Hour
Abundant Christianity

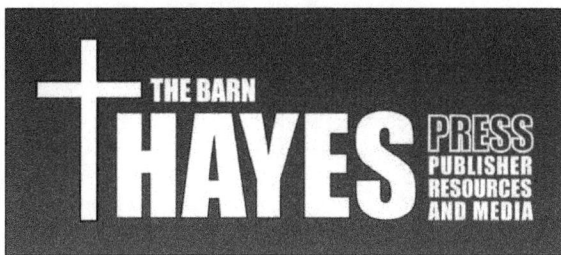

About the Publisher

Hayes Press (www.hayespress.org) is a registered charity in the United Kingdom, whose primary mission is to disseminate the Word of God, mainly through literature. It is one of the largest distributors of gospel tracts and leaflets in the United Kingdom, with over 100 titles and hundreds of thousands despatched annually. In addition to paperbacks and eBooks, Hayes Press also publishes Plus Eagles Wings, a fun and educational Bible magazine for children, and Golden Bells, a popular daily Bible reading calendar in wall or desk formats. Also available are over 100 Bibles in many different versions, shapes and sizes, Bible text posters and much more!

www.ingramcontent.com/pod-product-compliance
Lightning Source LLC
Chambersburg PA
CBHW021219020426
42331CB00003B/374